ANCIENT TOWN
OF
HIGH RENOWN

RHYMES AND POEMS FROM
DINGLE
TOWN AND PENINSULA

COMPILED BY
TOM FOX

Tom Fox
3/1/98

HOLY STONE

First published in 1997 by
Holy Stone Publications
The Mall, Dingle, Co. Kerry, Ireland.

© Tom Fox 1997

British Library Cataloguing in Publication Data
is available for this book.
ISBN 0 9528278 1 6

Cover design and typesetting by Tom Fox
Ink drawings by David O'Mahony
Printed by Colour Books Ltd, Dublin

CONTENTS

INTRODUCTON

This collection of rhymes, poems and the odd song came together as a result of the publication of the two photographic collections, Dingle Down The Years. While gathering the old photographs, very often a poem was located amongst them. The owners had the same regard for the poem as they had for the photograph. Over the seven years that I have been collecting I accumulated a large collection of poems. As I began compiling the book in late Autumn this year many more came into my possession.

Most of the poems are written by Dingle people but the pen of the visitor is included as well. They are all written from the heart by people who have a great grá for the people and the place. The poems will take you on a journey through the peninsula and will help you to reminisce about people, places and events in the Dingle Peninsula.

I wish to express my thanks to all the authors who gave me permission to include their poems in my book. Thanks to everybody who provided me with material and to all of you who have a great interest in my collections. It would not have been done without you. You can be as proud of these as I am myself.

Tom Fox,
The Mall,
Dingle.
November 1997

OLD DINGLE BY THE SEA

Old Dingle! dear old Dingle!
    Tho' I am far from thee;
I often sit and ponder,
    On day's that used to be.

And thro' an exiles dreaming,
    I watch the flowing tide;
Thy Lighthouse ever beaming,
    Across the ocean wide.

I see old Cnoc a Cairn,
    And distant Conor Hill;
The Grove beside the Churchyard,
    The river by the Mill.

Thy Convent and thy Chapel,
    Beside thy shady Green;
The school, the nuns, my schoolmates,
    I recollect each scene.

Thy Hospital of Mercy,
    Which overlooks the town;
Its nuns, whose noble life work,
    Is worthy of a crown.

Thy Monastery, its schoolrooms,
    The Courthouse by its side,
Thy mountain-girdled harbour,
    With its blue and rippling tide.

I visit thy dear homesteads,
    By road and street and sea;
And wonder if my old friends,
    Are there to welcome me.

The few I meet, I greet them,
　　They sadly, sadly say-
Those hands I'd clasp in friendship,
　　Are folded now in clay.

They're gone beyond all sorrow,
　　Beyond all woe and wail;
Beyond this world's tempests,
　　And shadows of the vale.

The teardrops fall in sadness,
　　And I bow beneath my woe;
While memory wreathes a garland,
　　O'er sleeping ones laid low.

I visit Nancy's Parlour,
　　And wish that I could be-
When seagulls call and dewdrops fall,
　　In Dingle o'er the sea .

Then back again I wander,
　　And gaze across at Reen;
Past the Tower and Lough and Station,
　　And home by old Cooleen.

The factory-whistle calling,
　　My dream is soon forgot;
Yet, it leaves a lingering sadness,
　　For that old familiar spot.

Tho' far away in exile,
　　My fancy often strays;
With memories of old Dingle,
　　And friends of bygone days.

Mary Glover

DINGLE TO 1936

I often think of my hometown
So many miles away,
That little place that nestles there
Alongside Dingle Bay.

In dreams I walk around the town
As I did long ago,
The Mall, Green Lane, the Holy Ground
Cooleen and Station Row.

And up Sráid Eoin and down again
And over the Spa Road,
And 'round by Coum and Baile Beag
To the small bridge once more.

I see again the Holy Stone,
The quay, the fishing fleet
And Cnoc a Chairn looking down
With Dingle at her feet.

The fun we had when we were young
I often time recall
The wran, the swimming in Slaidín,
The bonfires and the fall.

Up to the railway station
To see the trains come in
The simple joys of my young days
Will never come again.

And laughing, shouting with delight
As garsúns always do
We'd tumble down the Barrack Height
On our way home from school.

We walked out to the races
The two days for the fun
We never thought of horses
And didn't care what won.

Last thing at night we'd round the town
Ere to our home we'd go
The Mall, the Canons corner
And the Holy Ground below.

I won't go back, 'twould break my heart
My friends have passed away
I'll leave my bones in Springfield, Mass.,
And not by Dingle Bay.

AN EXILE REMEMBERS

On New Years Eve at midnight hour,
The band came down Main Street,
Jim Crone's big drum to the fore
Beat time for marching feet.

They played The Mall, The Holy Ground,
The Colony Gate, The Quay,
They kept alive a custom,
And welcomed New Year's Day.

For these good men were Dingle's soul,
They did it all for free,
And when they played the fife and drum,
They played for you and me.

They marched back home to the Holy Stone,
And we gave them a hearty cheer,
As they played once more for their very own,
To wish them a bright New Year.

AN EXILE'S MEMORIES

Ah, 'tis often, very often, when we're roaming far from home,
'Mid the pleasure of the stranger, that our recollections roam
To the days and hours and minutes, that were happy, glad and free,
Spent 'mongst dear old friends and kindly, in old Dingle by the sea.

In the stranger's land there is pleasure, there is joy and fun galore,
There are stout big hearts to greet you as you step upon their floor,
But those kindly souls and happy hearts do not appeal to me,
Like the happy-hearted gang I knew, in Dingle by the sea.

Sure 'twas there the ways were easy and the devilment was strong,
And the porter-barrel orators proclaimed the right and wrong,
With the famous Jackeen Donoghue proudly preaching liberty,
To the laughing crowds that listened, in old Dingle by the sea.

Ah, the Donoghues were great old stock; they proved it time and time,
Sure they plastered homes in no time, using mud instead of lime,
And while "Puddin", Tim and "Birdie" never sobered, poor Maggie
In her raiments grand and glowing went to church anear the sea.

And "Paiste" Lynch, God rest her soul, may Heaven be her bed,
'Twere many things her tongue did say were better left unsaid,
Yet, her fights with Biddy Bushell will ne'er forgotten be
By the scattered sons and daughters,from old Dingle by the sea.

And the "Holystone Conventions" held in old Pat Mara's flat,
Where the Aristocrats of Goat Street in consultations sat,
And where necks and skulls were broken, the wonder was to me,
That no one was ever murdered, in old Dingle by the sea.

Yes, I've heard "The Rakes of Mallow" and "The Peeler and the Goat"
On the violin and piano, and enjoyed them every note,
But poor old Naffy's penny flute impressed far more on me,
The soothing charms of music, in old Dingle by the sea.

When he'd "wet" his flute with porter, 'twas the signal to begin
And 'twas he could time the music to the tread of marching men,
And 'twas he could raise the cockles in the heart of you and me,
God be with you, Naff the Piper, in your grave beside the sea.

Of those mem'ries unforgotten, how oftimes I recall,
The figure of Seán Mara with his feet and legs and all,
His head going one direction, but his feet could ne'er agree,
'Till the Peelers fixed the "argument", in Dingle by the sea.

And Miss Hussey with her prayer book; she was old as Father Dan,
In the Chapel with but candlelight, she ever prayed for man,
Sure the sinners in the barony were cared well by three,
By Miss Hussey and Mike Moran and Miss Manning by the sea.

And the Poarchers and the Tar-boys and the hunters on the hill,
There was Connor John and Tommy Ned and other names that thrill,
Sure they could tar the Licence Boards and scatter shutters free,
Just as good as any men who tried, in Dingle by the sea.

And the honest Murty Boland, he could tell the damnedest lies,
And could read the Bible backways- sure he proved it to the boys-
Sure no wedding, wake or christening could e'er successful be,
If brave Murty wasn't present, in old Dingle by the sea.

And when we wanted penknives, sure we always bought one make,
'Twas the kind we bought and paid for, from poor Dan Wide Awake,
When he handed you the penknife, he would add, just gratis free,
A curse or two on your old bones, in old Dingle by the sea.

The Lady of the Townland, always dressed in perfect style,
Was the one and only Mary Trant, the sunshine of whose smile,
Sent the rays of joy and happiness,- when she wasn't on a spree,
Through the hearts of the old Bachelors, in old Dingle by the sea.

And then there was the Bogey-man, who scratched himself all day,
When hauling trunks for Travellers, on the mail or down the quay,
Ah, 'twas many a time and many, that he hunted Joe and me,
When we banged his door with bricks and stones, in old Dingle by the sea.

And I mind me of the visits of that little Jewman Mose,
To Mrs. Cox on John Street, who'd place porkchops on his nose,
Until poor Mose disgusted got, and thought 'twould better be,
To find some other customers, in old Dingle by the sea.

Lil Moran too, I don't forget, with "one leg in and out",
Sure he'd dance the Jigs and Hornpipes for but a pint of stout,
And he'd tell you of the stories of the things that used to be,
In the olden days of history, in old Dingle by the sea.

I hear again the Bellman, old Jim Stout who ne'er did fail,
To announce the great big meetings in the language of the Gael,
And t'was he that was well able, so I'm sure you'll all agree,
Jim Stout was quite a character, in old Dingle by the sea.

And the travellers and their donkeys and their soldering irons too,
And their pots and leaking saucepans,which they soldered up with glue,
And then the "Holy Ructions", which followed their big spree,
When the pots and pans were mended, in old Dingle by the sea.

Ah, I've heard the greatest songsters that the world ever knew,
And I've listened almost spellbound to their ringing voices true,
But the good old ballad singers, far more happy they made me,
With their martial songs on "Emmet" in old Dingle by the sea.

And the Patterns and the Races and the Pies and crubeens too,
And " the black man in the barrel"; and the Bully Maggies" new,
And "Find the little Double", those are mem'ries dear to me,
Tho' they cost me many shillings, in old Dingle by the sea.

I can ne'er forget the Pattern in Cloghane some years ago,
When we swiped and stole the honey, at whose house I do not know,
But Tommy Ned and Manning James, their honey they gave to me,
And it melted in my pockets, far from Dingle by the sea.

And the brave big Mrs Sweeney, ah, 'twas she could kheen and cry,
At the loss of some poor neighbour, whose time had come to die,
And she'd march and tramp to churchyards, yet her question e'er would be,
"Whose the man or child I'm crying for?", in old Dingle by the sea.

So, Mikeen Lyons is living still, as "thin" is he as yore,
Well, I mind me how we robbed him of Woodbine fags galore,
And we'd give him Swedish money, what e'er our purchase be,
For he was too fat to hunt us, in old Dingle by the sea.

There's Seán and Dickeen Baker and Mike Mullock aroo,
And "Putty" and Ned Connor, the toughest pair I knew,
And Paddy Bawn from John Street, they in mind come back to me,
They made life and times worth living for, in Dingle by the sea.

And the famous old Joan Kearney to our town was no disgrace,
Yet while living near the fountain, she never washed her face,
She could holler for the Peelers tho' when "Champion" acting free
Broke the Kearney cups and saucers, in Dingle by the sea.

And there's the greatest character who lived upon the Quay,
His nickname it was "Bushy" his real name I can't say,
He drank more Murphys porter and made more countries free
Than anyone who blessed himself, in Dingle by the sea.

I mind how children used to flee and into rat holes creep,
When e'er the town was visited by the tough-eyed Mickey Sweep,
With his brooms upon his shoulders; we felt daring tough and free,
And we plastered him with snowballs, in old Dingle by the sea.

On that sage old man Bill Darcy, tricks were played upon galore,
E'en the coffins of Tom Lynch's were placed against his door,
'Tis often times I've wondered how sane he e'er could be,
'Mongst the "devilmenting blackguards",in old Dingle by the sea.

And the "agile" Johnny Carthy, sure when he walked down the street,
You could always guess the weather by the movements of his feet,
Ah, those famous shoes of Johnny's in a museum kept should be,
For there could be nothing funnier, in old Dingle by the sea.

You may travel all America, from shore to distant shore,
But by our scattered exiles you'll find none respected more,
Than the man who led the beagles o'er mountain, gleann and lea,
Dick Thomas e'es a credit, in old Dingle by the sea.

And of course there are the Peelers, the scum of Irelands breed,
Those traitors to their motherland, who'd spurn a Nations creed,
Who'd tight the chains of Slavery, and stifle Liberty,
But their day is done in Ireland, and in Dingle by the sea.

But there are many others whom just now I can't recall,
Who have added fame and glory, added honour one and all,
To the famous "Gascan" stronghold, more than a memory
To the exiled Sons and Daughters of old Dingle by the sea.

There are happier days acoming to those longing hearts that wait,
For the Freedoms Dawn in Erin, for the Opening of the Gate,
To the fields of Peace and Happiness and to full-fledged Liberty
For that God-blessed Land of Erin, and old Dingle by the sea.

Slaudeen.

DINGLE

As I look down from Greenmount
Upon the harbour scene,
I cannot but stand still and gaze
At beauty all men must praise.

The tourists speed on road below
And miss what now I see:
A little town at the water's edge
Sheltered by hills serene.

Brandon and Blasket beckon on,
They call and call and claim
A rugged and splendid shore and sea
And, yes, they deserve that fame.

But see, the harbour, the pier, the hills,
The church, the roads, the streets:
Are the cradle, the nurse, the place, the scene
Where the Father first called me to be.

Sr. Canice Barrett.

FAREWELL TO DINGLE

So I bid farewell to Dingle,
Your like I ne'er will see,
On foreign soil I spent a while,
To dwell my memories.

Those memories of my childhood,
As it was long years ago,
By The Mall, Green Lane, The Holy Ground,
Spa Road and Station Row.

'Twas sad the day we parted,
My true love by my side,
And sailed away from my home town,
Across the ocean wide.

With laughter, sport and pleasure,
They were our only rules,
We'd stroll the Banks to Slaudeen,
For a bathe in the ocean pool.

Our youthful days we passed away,
With little work or care,
The Sráid Eoin Wren,The Green and Gold,
The Goat Street and The Quay.

But, alas our dream was broken,
No work we found at home,
So we left one November's morning
A distant land to roam.

COOLEEN

Oh! Glorious Dingle looking so serene,
I have roamed the world over your likes I have ne'er seen,
They talk about their holidays of sunshine and of skiing,
I'd rather one day in Dingle and a walk in Cooleen.

Out the banks to the rocks in Slaudeen,
Watching the hills across in Cahirciveen,
The fishing boats returning since early morning dawn,
Passing home by the lighthouse and the old Towereen Bán.

The seagulls singing their songs of joy,
Being fed with fish as they pass by,
No lovelier sight has yet to be seen,
Than sailing home by lovely Cooleen.

While Fungi jumps about the sea,
Visitors clap their hands with glee,
This little fish has changed our plans,
Has brought us tourists from far off lands.

They come from countries far away,
To sail their boats out Dingle Bay,
Not one in Dingle would change that scene,
That would take from our walk 'round lovely Cooleen.

On through the town to the beautiful west,
Where the Sleeping Giant is always at rest,
The beautiful sunset right down on our shore,
Casting its rays of colour over sweet Dún an Óir.

Clogher Strand with its sisters so high,
Silhouetting the western sky,
At the top of the Maum, what a sight to be seen,
Of my famous walk around lovely Cooleen.

Visitors come and natives go,
Some never again to be seen,
But memories of Dingle will always remain,
Of their walk around lovely Cooleen.

Cáit Curley,
10th. Feb. 1995.

MEMORIES OF YOUTH

Did you live in Dingle in the days of yore,
When the key was left in every door,
You shared the table with those within,
Be it tinkerman or wealthy king.

Work and money was hard to find,
Understanding neighbours were always kind,
We sang and danced and enjoyed a yarn,
"Wit was a gift" and some had the charm.

Every street had a character of its own,
From the top of John Street to the Holy Stone,
At each corner they would congregate,
Exchanging views at night so late.

Those were the days, the days of yore,
With memories full of many more,
Our simple youth was hard to beat,
Where we played our games out on the street,
Those were the days, the days of yore,
We spent in Dingle by the shore.

Cáit Curley.

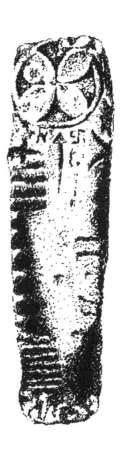

Aglish Stone

THE FORGE

God rest you Tommy Barry,
And Sean and William too,
For shelter in your friendly forge
When winds up Bridge Street blew.

We stood upon the narrow path,
Against the white washed wall
Until the clouds came overhead,
And the rain began to fall.

That was the time to move inside
And meet the warm glow
There always was a welcome
In summer or in snow.

Some sat inside the window,
The cold one's sought the hob,
The smoker's shared a Woodbine
For no one had a bob.

Those were the hungry thirties,
No work for man or boy,
No money in their pockets,
Their best years slipping by.

One would step out and grasp the sledge
To lend a helping hand
And weld upon the anvil,
The red-hot iron band.

Another blew the bellows,
While Tommy raked the fire,
And soon the slack shone bright again,
The horseshoes funeral pyre.

And then the banks were opened,
For England needed more
Workers in her factories
While she prepared for war.

For war was surely coming,
The signs were plain as day,
The forge youth got the message
And for work they went away.

Goodbyes were said, some tears were shed,
The train was on its way,
A last look o'er the racecourse
Their loved ones in Dingle Bay.

Some came back, some ne'er returned,
Some lie in foreign graves,
Far from the Forge and Holy Ground,
And carefree boyhood days.

Maurice McKenna

WHAT I REMEMBER OF DINGLE 1920's & 1930's

The fishermen on Hudson's Bridge
Dressed in their navy blue,
Muintir na Rinne Bige
I lift my hat to you.

You tacked across the harbour's mouth
On foggy winter nights,
Before you hit the moorings
And saw the cottage lights.

O'Flaherty's, Grahams and Devanes
And other Reen Beags too,
Were borne home to Burnham
To the graveyard 'neath Carhoo.

CASEY'S HOTEL

Oh!, I roamed into Dingle one evening last May,
Having tramped all the ways from the fair at Glenbeigh,
I was hungry and tired and my pockets were light
And I had no tea ration or lodging for the night.

I searched around Goat Street in hope to get a place,
And from that onto John Street in huff and disgrace,
And into Mikie Casey and says he "It is all right
But mind you must pays me one shilling a night".

Oh! Dear Mikie Casey, you do not fear God
And where in the blazes would I find one bob,
I wouldn't mind if it was eight pence and that was alright,
But there is devil the likes of your shilling a night.

Oh! Dear Mikie Casey, I will have you to know,
If the workhouse was going, it is there I would go,
For a bath and a clean shirt, wouldn't that be allright,
But there is devil the likes of your shilling a night.

Oh! Dear Mikie Casey, 'tis known fine well,
That you keep the worst Scratch from the Blaskets to Hell,
You have green bugs and red bugs, and some black and white,
And they ate Paddy Moriarty and the shilling a night.

Oh! Me lads I was hungry, 'tis true to relate,
I went to bed twelve stone, came down only eight,
For the bugs they attacked me, with bite after bite,
And they drank my blood dry in the shilling a night.

Oh! I woke the next morning, I rose nearly wild,
My heart was as black as the kettle was boiled,
For I cursed Mikie Casey, to Hell and Daylight,
And I'll never return to the - Shilling a Night.

Rory Ward.

RECALL

Now, I look down from Brandon
And see the Maharees,
Veiled in the haze of summer,
Sleeping in the waveless seas.

And now I feel the wind come
From the slopes of Glandilay,
And the silver girdled islands,
Jade green in Brandon Bay.

And I look south from Brandon
To where the Scorid falls,
To Lough Adoon's dark waters
And lilts and chants and calls.

And calls me home forever,
For home can never be
But the hills of Corca Dhuibhne
Lapped in a timeless sea.

James Barrett

SWEET ANCIENT TOWN OF DINGLE, KERRY

Sweet ancient town of high renown,
I love your craggy mountains,
Your snow capped hills, your running rills,
Your noble lakes and fountains.
I love your streets, your cool retreats,
Your boughs and shady arbours,
Your lonely vales and rosebloom dales,
Your noble lakes and borders.
I love the Scragg, that snowcapped crag,
Where the banshee sang enchanted,
Her weird low moan, and dear ochone,
O'er Cairn Hill thats haunted.

I love the green where could be seen,
The bell-shaped Rose of Sharon,
'Midst lonely glades and pleasant fades,
Amongst the thistle and hawthorn.
I love the Banks where I played pranks,
By Cooleen's glittering waters,
Gathering shells and fairy bells,
To deck Dingle's fairest daughters.
I love the grove where the maidens rove,
In hope to meet their lovers,
To have a talk and a pleasant walk,
Beneath the oak that covers.
The maidens blush, the young mans hush,
The daisies and the clover,
And the little stalks and pleasant walks,
The birds around them hover.

I love John Street, where the good monks meet,
To chant sweet heavenly praises,
To God on high, who's always nigh,
To shower on them his graces.
I love Green Lane, that hallowed plain,
Where convent school and chapel,
Are standing there in solemn air,
To fight for Christ his battle.
And you need not fret that I'll forget,
The Holy Stone and Orchard,
And that little cot where the boys played flatts,
In the grand hotel of Meara's.

But now, mo bhrón, I am far from home,
I am a lonely distant stroller,
That was banished from my fathers home,
Until my manhood years were over.
Where e'er I roam, I'll think of home,
The playmates of my childhood,
The dance, the goal, the flowing bowl,
My rambles in the wild wood.

In dreams I see those dear to me,
Collectively and single,
In tents so gay on Lady's Day,
The patron day of Dingle.

I'd like to see once more, mo chroí,
Your cliff bound bays and harbours,
Your towering creeks and craggy peaks,
Your glens and bowery arbours.
May you, O Lord, grant this reward,
To me, whose only pleasure,
Would be to see, Old Ireland free,
Our grandest, chiefest, treasure.
So now you see, we'll all agree,
And get some priest to bind us,
Into an oath that can't be broke,
'Till we break the chains that entwine us.
So now my boys, lets all rejoice,
And all unite and mingle,
And always boast and drink a toast,
To those sweet colleens that left sweet Dingle.

The above poem was composed by Ed Smith from a postcard view of Dingle which he received in Holyoke, Mass., USA. He was born in Castlegregory, Co. Kerry, in 1840, became a monitor school teacher and taught in the Blasket Island. Later he emigrated to the States. He was connected with the Board of Education in Holyoke, but was retired from the same when I met him about 1913, his age was then 73. He was a native speaker, and remembered the Land League days in Dingle and Ballyferriter, and was a personal friend of Padraig Ferriter, the national secretary of the Dingle branch, even though he was a native of Ballyoughtreac, Ballyferriter, which then had its original name- the parish of Dunurlin.

Mise le mór meas,
Kruger Kavanagh, Dunquin.
26th March, 1966

THE TWO BLACK KERRY COWS

The Ferriter peelers were boycotted well,
For to them not one in the townland would sell,
So out of sheer pity, those quellers of rows
Received from Lord Ventry two black Kerry cows.

An emergency man from the County Mayo
With two strapping peelers to Burnham did go,
They were all gaily singing their spirits to rouse
While marching behind the two Kerry cows.

But trudging along made the poor fellows dry
And they all felt inclined for a drop on the sly,
So they quietly sat down a carouse to begin
In that neat little mansion, Dan Kennedy's Inn.

While each hero was drinking to strengthen his heart
The two Kerries outside took a notion to start,
One started due east and the other due west
While the bailiff and peelers were taking their rest.

The bailiff was first to discover the loss
And in chasing the Kerry he got a big toss
In a pool of foul water that chanced to be near,
For his poor brain was muddled with Kennedy's beer.

After struggling hard he got rid of the pool
And he felt his poor carcass exceedingly cool,
Then he ran to the inn with the speed of the hare
To summon the peelers still drinking in there.

And one he persuaded to give up his rest
And they chased the black Kerry that started due west,
Not a trace of the Kerry was seen anywhere,
Like the witches of old it sailed off in the air.

And the peeler being tipsy too fell in the pool,
In his rage he then called the poor bailiff a fool,
Started back to his friend to continue to revel
And the black Kerry cow he consigned to the devil.

DINGLE

I often think of Dingle as a place where time stands still,
The Harbour and the fishing boats - the Tower on Burnham Hill,
The Lighthouse on the headland - walks along the shore,
The Dolphin diving in the bay - and places to explore!

The Holy Stone in Goat Street - the churchyard of Saint James,
The Library, the Courthouse, and the bookshop down the lane,
The Races - the Regatta - the Mall on market day,
A glass of stout with Foxy John - the Wrenboys on their way!

The Conor Pass - Ventry Strand - the road around Slea Head,
The Blaskets, stately, calm, aloof - and Coumeenole ahead!
The winding path to Dunquin pier - the waves on Clogher Beach,
Sybil with her Sisters - and Mount Brandon out of reach!

Softly spoken Gaelic - tales of ships that sailed from Spain,
The ancient church of Gallarus - and fuchsia in the rain.
A school of glistening black canoes stranded at Dooneen,
And Brendan's voyage from Brandon Creek for Paradise Unseen!

Ted Creedon

NANCY BROWN'S PARLOUR

At eve when the sun with diamonds crown
The azure brow of Dingle Bay,
I love to visit Nancy Brown's
To while an hour away.

The parlour has no upholstery,
Save a lounge without cushion or spring;
Yet, how pleasant there to be
And hear the billows sing.

And there is no piano,
On which to render staves,
But music grand, in their furious flow,
Is furnished by the waves.

How interesting 'tis to read
The initials on the wall;
Of men - some exiles, some dead -
Who've paid Nancy a call.

Or gaze upon the heaving expanse,
Where revel monsters of the deep,
While on the waves the sun-rays dance,
As to the shore they leap.

To them I say, who in their quest
Visit places of renown,
Of seeing nature at its best,
Go visit Nancy Browns.

A DINGLE RAMBLE

One evening fine with hasty feet
I left a busy Dingle street,
Discontented till I stood
Beneath the shade of Burnham wood.

When reclining on a grassy dell
I heard Coláiste Íde's bell,
Saw lowing cows return from a field,
Anxious their daily milk to yield.

Reenbeg's Hill looked grey and steep
Where sailors of the Armada sleep,
Their last repose on this lonely ground
Awaiting Gabriel's bugle sound.

A thrush struts across the College lawn
Practising her preludes to the dawn,
Promising saplings quelled my fears,
The woods won't vanish with the years.

At Raheenyhooig 'mid cypress and yew
Are the last resting places of friends I knew,
Arousing thoughts I shall not spurn,
Memories that please and some that burn.

Mount Brandon holds last rays of day
Where Brendan used retire to pray,
Long since he and his monks are gone
But in this height his name lives on.

On homeward journey I paused awhile
Where a stone stands from the town a mile,
A huge boulder revered by druids and sages
In the dark and distant ages.

From here I see the Dingle Green
Resplendent in its summer sheen,
High above the trees and chimneys tall
The parish church towers over all.

Milltown village is quite still
Without the rumble of its water mill,
Up the river near the quivering reeds
The silver salmon unmolested feeds.

Dingle Harbour with its surrounding hills
With rapture the beholder fills,
Across the smooth water I see the land
Edged by rough shingle and golden sand.

Adorned by an ancient tower,
Oft times my refuge from a passing shower,
Its stony walls hold firm and fast
Against summer's heat and winter's blast.

Tigh an tSoluis hasn't shown its beacon light
To warn its sea travellers in the night,
Of caves and rocks which won high renown
For the legendary mermaid, Nancy Brown.

Oft was she seen combing her golden hair
As she basked in the crispness of the morning air,
Sailors seeing the human yet fishy form
Always reckoned on a coming storm.

It is now the hour when daylight dies,
The sun sinks low in the Blasket skies,
Knockacairn wears a pall of cloud
And Greenmount lies in mist enshroud.

The fishing boats return from the bay
Where they ploughed the waters the lifelong day,
Fifty footers without sail or oar,
How loudly, yet smoothly their engines roar.

I thought of friends across the foam
That through these scenes no longer roam,
Living in cities of great fame
They think of Dingle just the same.

Brendan Foley, March 1955

THE DINGLE FISHING FLEET

I stood on Cooleen as the summers dawn,
Was brightening o'er sweet Beenbawn,
Painting the cloudlets with a rosy red,
O'er its bleak and windswept head.

Soon I heard the rhythm of the oars,
With voices from the pier and shores,
Where the boats at anchor lay,
Before proceeding to old Dingle Bay.

On that June morning they looked so fine,
From the mastheads to the waterline,
Hulls and wheelhouses painted with every hue,
Drenched with the dawn's crystal dew.

Skilful hands that shoot every trawl and net,
Till the sun in the western sea has set,
With powerful engines in full motion,
Reaping the rich harvest of the ocean.

Pleasant for those on Lough's and Slaidin's side,
To see them homeward bound at eventide,
Filling the hearts with justifiable pleasure,
To see them laden with "God's own treasure."

The fleet of former years had no engine but sail,
From Dingle harbour to Bantry and Kinsale,
More distant places - Howth, Killybegs, County Donegal,
The Aran Islands and Galway all were ports of call.

Furnished with experience and seaman's lore,
The hardy toilers knew no more,
And looked towards the constant Northern Star,
To guide them safely from afar.

And prayed to One who controlled the petrels flight,
To steer them safely in the starless night
From the dangers of the deep,
The submerged rock and treacherous reef.

Industrious, fearless fishermen I knew so well,
Providential escapes they could dramatically tell,
When the billows raged white with foam
And they at sea so far from home.

The tempest veering from the "Norid" to the south,
Obscuring familiar landmarks and the harbours mouth,
Anxious kinfolk peering through the maine,
Hidden in sheets of spray, and rain.

For residents of Strand Street, The Quay and Holy Ground,
The tread of heavy leather seaboots at dawn was a familiar sound,
For the wearers it was no pleasant sight to see,
The fleet becalmed like painted ships on a painted sea.

Leaving Cooleen's rustic and peaceful shore,
I thought of gallant sailing days of yore,
Well trimmed ketch-rigged hookers old Dingle's pride,
Receding in the mist of memory's tide.

Life's voyage is symbolic of a fishing boat,
Battling with life's storms to keep afloat,
Appealing to the merciful Master who calmed the sea,
On that blessed night in Galilee.

Brendan Foley

AT MULLAGHVEAL AT EVENTIDE

Popular pastimes I oft forsake,
To seek the solitude of Mullaghveal Lake,
Fishing from a buoyant boat,
Where water lilies gently float.

Where pleasant hours do quickly fly
Like swallows in a summer sky,
My heart then fills with thoughts of home
As Venus appears in Heavens dome.

When the fox emerges from his den
In silence of the brackened glen,
In answer to the curlews call
O'er the Pedlars silvery waterfall.

The willow warbler bids departing day farewell
In unison with the far sea swell,
From leafy sallies wrapt in gloom
Till the rising of the majestic moon.

Evening casts a veil of purple hue
On hills at noon were grey and blue,
And on jagged crags where black faced sheep,
O'er the heather clad vale, a vigil keep.

The heron is contemplating her solo flight,
To wade in shadows of the darkening light,
In a hidden world so peaceful and so calm,
In a fragrant atmosphere, like soothing balm.

Poet, angler, artist understand
Why I love this lake fashioned by nature's hand,
On whose bosom man will soon realise
The peace of Eden beyond the skies.

While winter reigns, I have my thoughts and dreams
Of a fish filled lough and rapid mountain streams,
Though Brandon's peak is white with snow
And water lilies in the lough no longer grow.

Yearning for the brightness of the catkined spring
And when the mayfly is on the wing,
Pink-tipped petals will there expand
On the crystal waters of this fairy land.

Brendan Foley.

THE DINGLE BEAGLE HUNT

Sweet it was for me to hear the beagles horn
In the stillness of an October morn,
The "Meet" was at the Holy Stone after early Sunday Mass,
To proceed to coverts of Glen's, Ballyhea or Conor Pass.

With wagging tails and heads down bent
The beagles seek a warm scent,
'Till followers hear the Master shout,
"Watch out, watch out - the hare is out."

The dogs run lively on the trail,
In pursuit of "Pus" o'er hill and dale,
The "Tallyho" mingles with loud bayings of the hounds,
The hills and glens echo with melody of their sounds.

The dogs are called off with blowing of the horn
When "Pus" returns to the bush where she was born,
For Dingle's humane beaglemen it was so rare
To see the kill of the noble hare.

Once a hard pressed hare made a sudden break
And swam Mullachaveals largest lake,
The huntsman cheered her with a thunderous roar
When she triumphantly reached the opposite shore.

They showed no mercy to Cullinagh's elusive fox
And gave chase to reynard on Ballinasig's hill and rock,
No great effort was made to save his life,
The enemy of the shepherd and farmers wife.

During King Phillips golden reign,
Sportsmen came from the sunny land of Spain,
"To the Hunt" toasts were drunk and Spanish songs were sung,
'Till the oaken rafters of Green Street's wine shops rung.

My hunting day's I boastfully did recall
When I saw a photo of beagles in a Dingle hall,
My heart was filled with pride and pleasure,
Moments of my hunting days I'll always treasure.

Brendan Foley '71

1953

It was the twenty-seventh of September,
The year was nineteen fifty-three,
From all over Ireland they came to Dublin,
The All-Ireland Final they came to see.

The teams competing were Armagh and Kerry
In a final they had not met before,
And eighty-five thousand packed that great arena
To see a game that is famous the country over.

From early morning the sun was shining
But on Croke Park cast a golden beam,
As the teams paraded in all their splendour,
The Saffron and White and the Gold and Green.

Seán Quinn of Armagh, Jas Murphy of Kerry
Were there to lead their men around,
And never before in the history of Éirinn
Was there so many people in so little ground.

Bishop Moynihan of the Kerry Diocese,
To throw in the ball, he was standing there.
As the Artane Boys Band played the National Anthem
And to tell the world was Mícheál Ó hÉithir.

The ball thrown in with Kerry cheering,
A start like this we hadn't seen before,
For in the second minute Jim Brosnan, Kerry,
Sent over the bar for the opening score.

Centre-half John Cronin sent in to Tadhg Lyne
Who proved to be a useful gun.
He placed Tom Ashe who sent straight and over,
The score board read two points to none.

Then a rolling ball came in from mid-field
And made its way to the Kerry net,
Roache and Foley looked at each other,
How it got there, they can't figure yet.

The ball kicked out, it went to Seán Murphy
Who sent the Kingdom to the attack again,
And Jackie Lyne sent in a low one
That was just cleared by the Armagh men.

An Armagh shot came in from mid-field
Towards the Kerry square it was seen to roll,
But the Kerry goalie, Johnnie Foley,
At the expense of a penalty he saved a goal.

The ball was placed by referee McDermott,
The man who that day wore a cap,
And for the Kingdom alone stood Foley
All, all alone in the Kerry Gap.

All was set save who was the taker,
Seán Quinn sent down McCorry Bill,
The Sam Maguire stood on the border,
And for a second Croke Park stood still.

The Armagh supporters their flags got ready,
To cheer once more that great Ulster side,
McDermott blew, McCorry drew,
And to our delight he had sent it wide.

Their hopes now shattered, they had lost their chances,
The Kingdom once more was to reign supreme
And the Sam Maguire was on its way to Kerry,
This time to make it Seventeen.

Jas Murphy's men now stood out in glory,
With style and speed such you never saw,
They had beaten Louth in the semi-final
And were on their way to defeat Armagh.

So throughout the Kingdom about that Final,
For many a year the story will be told,
How Armagh kept defending
Though their lines were bending
Before the final onslaught of the Green and Gold.

Patrick O'Connor.

FROM COUMDUBH TO GLENAHOO

I know it was Sir Edmund
Climbed the peaks near Kathmandu,
But did he climb the mountain range
That rise over Glenahoo.

If you come to Dingle
Don't sit there with a glass,
See Mount Eagle and Mount Brandon
Or walk out the Conor Pass.

We have a group to guide you
Or put you to the test,
For walking on the mountains
They are the very best.

When I saw them on the clifftop,
Though the number it was small,
I thought they were some Gurka's
From the mountains of Nepal.

They walked along a mountain trail
Winding through the purple heath,
Where the mighty cliffs dip sheer against
The peaceful lakes beneath.

Around each shadowy peak above
Where the hare and reynard lie,
And the ravens flew like specks of black
Across the evening sky.

They stopped at the altar of the penal days,
They stopped at the waterfall
To see the leaping trout on the lake below
That feeds the river Scaul.

Then with careful grace they walked along
With slow unhurried tread,
They gazed down on the valleys
And on the mountains overhead.

Until they reached a lofty peak
That looked into Maghanaboe,
They saw it like a serpent
Its valley river flow.

What beauty and what wonder,
Like a job of work well done,
Two mighty walls of mountain,
As if reaching to the sun.

They walked into the valley,
They said they would rest awhile,
And then they would trace the river
Like Livingstone traced the Nile.

The mountain lambs were bleating,
It was August of the year,
They sat for some refreshments
Out in the mountain air.

The mountains they looked mighty,
Yet the valley was so green,
But they brought their movie camera
To capture all the scene.

For when the time will tick away,
As time will come and go,
They can see it again in later years,
Their walk through Maghanaboe

I know most of those mountains,
Highest peak or lowly mound,
It was here I spent some happy days
When I ran with hare and hound.

Some talk about the Himalaya
Or a tropical lagoon
But give me the view from the mountain top
That rise over Loch Adoon.

Take our youth out to the mountains,
Show them nature at its best,
Away from the world of Dallas,
Dynasty or Falcon Crest.

We have many mountains
But our mountaineers are few,
So come out and walk it sometime
From Coumdubh to Glenahoo.

Patrick O'Connor.

FUNGIE

When I look from my window, I view a pleasant scene,
I see a lone wild friendly dolphin swim from the lighthouse to Slaudeen,
I see him swim across to Burnham in view of Dingle Town,
Then out around the Crow Rock and back to Nancy Browne.

He is in the Dingle Harbour for the past five years or more,
The fishermen they saw him then, they saw but knew no more,
He came to greet them in the morning on their way to the fishing ground
And was so playful in the evening when they were homeward bound.

John O'Connor went to swim with him and thought he was so tame,
One day he called him Fungie and he answered to that name,
Then a few more came to swim with him and his bottle nose to rub,
Brian and Shiela came from England and the Tralee Sub Aqua Club.

The tourists got attracted, he was a part of Dingle now,
They saw him swim alongside the boat or leap before the bow,
They came in smaller numbers then but now they come in mobs,
Publicised by Heathcote Williams or the famous Dr. Dobbs.

He has cured the ills of many without any charge or fuss,
Small farmers in the tax net or others in distress,
Hospitals are now closing, medical cards are hard to get,
So, your only hope is Fungie if any ailment you should get.

Now go and see Small Martin and he will put you right,
His name could shine in Harley St., if the dredger won't cause his flight,
He will take you to the dolphin ground where you dive and swim at will
And you are cured before you know it without a tablet or a pill.

Reports of cures are coming in, I hope they aren't lies,
Cripples are now walking, more are reading with glass eyes,
So if you are on the waiting list for a wish bone or a hip,
Just go down and swim with Fungie, you need only have a dip.

How he came to Dingle is anybody's bet,
He could be sent from Heaven to help clear the National Debt,
So, if he is caught out in a storm and he seeks the shelter of the Lough,
He will be guided by Big Paddy with his Beacon on the Rock.

Politicians didn't bring him and for that we must applaud,
In a Gaeltacht town like Dingle his name could be Dorád,
But the name it doesn't matter if he stays in Dingle Bay,
You know Health Cuts were a factor in the demise of Charles J.

Patrick O'Connor.

A TRIBUTE TO THE WEST KERRY TEAM

At last, at last we have it back
After a long and weary wait.
The last time that we saw the Cup
Was in nineteen forty eight.

We stood to cheer the Dingle team
As the final whistle blew.
We had cycled in from Dingle,
There was no other way to go.

Tom Long went up to take the Cup,
Five times they had won before.
How long we had to wait again
Until nineteen eighty four.

The year before we had no bike,
The journey it was far.
At first we were going to walk it
But we took the horse and cart.

They were the men to follow,
The greatest ever seen.
They won in the Dingle colours,
They won in the Gold and Green.

Most came in by bicycle,
Because there was no train
But we came in our little horse and cart
And got their just the same.

Then the war was over
And to progress we did yield.
We rooted out the fairy fort
And put a wall around the field.

An old man in his eighties
To the sportsfield paid a trip.
Said, "If you touch the fairies,
You are through with the Championship"

I hope you believe my story
For it is no fairy tale.
Sometime later it was stated
That the sportsfield was for sale.

Then along came Gabriel Casey,
A young teacher from Lispole.
I think he spoke in Gaelic,
The words he used were "Fan go fóill".

I can lead a winning team
From Kerry's rugged west.
If we only pull together
And forget the feuding past.

Paddy Browne was there to write it down
And as he wished them well,
Said, "First we must get guidance
From this man we call John L".

Then turning to Sinn Connor,
Said, "Remember Uncle Bill!
He'd be the man for Jacko,
Sadly, he's not with us still".

But Vincent did the needy,
He was outstanding on the day,
The only man in Ireland
To master Jacko Shea.

Sullivan was the keeper
But he didn't stand alone,
For he was well protected
By Bernard from Sráid Eoin.

Fit and fighting Roibeárd Casey
Would keep going until he'd die.
A professor and respected
By his cares in Mary I.

Sayers and Moriarty they
contested every ball,
As did their famous club mates,
The Doyles from Anascaul.

Healy from the Castle,
Fitzgerald from Moorestown,
When they linked up with Mansell
The scores man wrote it down.

South Kerry kept attacking
Until the call of time
But every time they tried it
Liam Connor cleared his line.

The West, the West, was now awake
This fairy spell had gone,
With Paud O'Shea and Jamesie
The star war sure was on.

Four in a row now is the aim
And that is no Kerry joke.
In the meantime we will be waiting
For another fairy stroke.

So we have won the County Championship
And if you are still alive
You will see Paud O'Shea
Lead the Green and Gold in 1985.

Patrick O'Connor.

THE YEAR EIGHTY FIVE

It was the year eighty five,
The sun it failed to shine,
It cleared the butter mountain
And they anti-freezed the wine.

No sun shone down, in country or town,
We had no golden grain,
The crops were tossed, the hay was lost
From months of constant rain.

We got our greatest fright when we saw the blight
And the bees stayed in the hive,
Would the humble spud, only now in bud,
Go as in forty five.

Farmers prayed to their God above,
Fine weather to them send,
And for those who quoted Colmcille,
It was the beginning of the end.

But there was a message very clear,
It was there for all to see,
That message came from the same great God
Through the statues in Asdee.

I went to Ballinspittle
And from there up to Asdee,
I didn't see the statues move
But the statues did move me.

Morale was down in country and town,
Our crops were in decay,
But the one bright spot, before we had our lot,
To be in Croke Park on All-Ireland day.

The giants of old, Old Moore foretold,
Would not be there to play,
But the very best, they laid to rest,
And were in Croke Park that day.

The Dublin Blue, well known to you,
As is the Gold and Green,
It was town against the country,
The Culchie against Jackeen.

In goal stood Charlie Nelligan,
Seán Walsh was centre way.
To his left was Mick Spillane,
To his right stood Paudie O'Shea.

The half back line stood the test of time,
Ger Lynch and Tommy Doyle,
At centre half stood Tom Spillane
Who showed some class and style.

But when the going got really tough,
Up to the clouds they rose,
The mighty hands of Jack O'Shea
Partnered by Ambrose.

That mountain hare called Pat Spillane,
He always did us proud,
We had Ogie in the forty
And one goal one from Timmy Dowd.

But it was the Bomber Liston
Who played havoc in the square,
Helping Power and Sheehy,
That man was everywhere.

Two twelve we had on the score board
But the Dubs they had two eight,
And though the time was ticking,
How long it was to wait.

Dwyer was getting anxious,
Would they pull it from the fire,
But there was no way that Paudie O'Shea
Would part with the Sam Maguire.

Paudie was the Captain,
That fearless Gaeltacht man,
He held his own man scoreless,
Then walked up to take the Sam.

It was Paudie then who brought it back
And left the Dubs to mourn their loss,
So the following day it was on display,
In his pub at Chapel Cross.

Patrick O'Connor.

THE RETURN OF FUNGIE

Snow showers were high in the morning sky,
The arctic winds they blew,
When Radio Kerry came on air,
It was Fool's Day nineteen ninety two.

How sad it was for Dingle
As the news flash did unfold,
That Fungie had left and gone away
Because of our greed for gold.

Did Moynihan take him to the lakes,
A thing he would like to do,
But if he crossed to Portmagee,
He is gone by Donoghue.

We have no power in Dingle
Since Begley went away,
We left him go, so now we know
And we have also lost C.J.

In Valencia they got ready
Their share of the gold to take,
While silent men in Dingle
Were preparing for the wake.

The boatmen went to Máire's,
How sad to see them cry,
Their boats tied up alongside the pier,
Their wet suits out to dry.

Oh! How we will miss you Fungie,
Have you left us in a huff,
They shed a tear as they sipped their beer,
They had clay pipes and snuff.

Small Martin looked across the bay,
Then said in sombre tones,
"I know that he will come back again,
I feel it in my bones".

Then came the welcome message
That he hadn't gone away,
Sure, it is many a cloudy morning
Brought forth a sunny day.

Patrick O'Connor.

THE ENVELOPE

The day the Irish walked on Everest
In May of ninety three,
More walked on Knocachairn
To keep their grazing free.

They came down from the mountains
And from Dingle town as well,
They spoke of Michael Davitt
And of Charles Stewart Parnell.

Keep a grip of all your holding
If a deed you have to show,
Let no one take your grazing,
That advice came long ago.

In glowing words a speaker told
How every acre counts,
And they listened as if listening
To the Sermon on the Mount.

The aid you will get from Europe
Will be determined there,
And your quota set in Brussels
For each acre or hectare.

They have made all areas equal
In valley or mountain slope,
So, the more you have the more you get
In your Brussels envelope.

So don't fence in your neighbour,
You could be playing with fire
And asked to take up any driven stake
Or take down any fencing wire.

It was then they held a meeting
To discuss or to decide
If this thing should be acted on
Or gently laid aside.

They knew it was important,
That it could affect the fate
Of grazing rights and rural life
In mountains small and great.

Before this aid from Europe
They paid their rent and rate
And lived a life with a smaller fund
But the quality was great.

They walked to school, then ran back home
To where they longed to be,
Out with the Meitheal in the cornfield
When they stopped for evening tea.

They went to mass in a horse and car,
A few in a pony and trap,
There was nine pence for the pictures then
And four for the dancehall hop.

There were stories told by young and old
When they came from near and far,
To take their place in the creamery queue
In a donkey or horse and car.

They walked the cattle to the fair,
They walked them across the hill
And dealt with jobbers who were out since dawn
In search of an early kill.

When the cattle were sold a ticket they got,
Then the jobber would point his cane,
A signal to walk with dog and stick
The cattle to the train.

But there was respect for Church and State
And morals were so high,
No need to lock the door at night
Or a spy up in the sky.

Gone are the potato and corn fields,
The meitheal is no more,
But instead a cheque from Brussels
In an envelope to the door.

Gone too are the sheep from the mountain top
The scotch high-mountain breed,
Where the farmer gazed, where his flock once grazed
And the grouse had ample feed.

Now the sheep are fed on expensive nuts
For gone is their heather and grass
And gone is the bark of the collie dog
Once heard on the mountain pass.

How strange the change that have come about
As we drift in the Euro tide,
The heather grazed off the mountain
And the prime land set aside.

So we live in the shadow of Europe now
And there may be no other hope,
But we look back with pride on a quality of life
We exchanged for the envelope.

Patrick O'Connor.

ST. MANCHAN'S LAMENT

Through the mist of time mans greatest crime
In his quest to feed the masses,
In his haste is laying the planet waste
With methane and clorofloro gases.

Each colour and breed showing signs of greed
And common sense to lack;
So now the ozone layer is showing signs of wear,
Have we time to turn back.

If you travel west from Dingle
And turn right at the timber mill,
A nicer view would be hard to see
Than the one from Baile Riabhach Hill.

Looking east from the Teampeall Geal
You can see its beauty there,
Where they must fight to maintain their right
To breathe God's own fresh air.

The monks of old who settled here,
We still hear their church bells chime,
For they have left us more than the standing stones
That have stood the test of time.

St. Manchan is buried in this sacred place
Beneath a standing stone
And proof that the saint is sleeping there
Is written down in ogham.

The pheasants fed in this beauty spot
Where wildlife does abound,
And curlews call from overhead
On the wing to the feeding ground.

The little streams they wind their way
To meet below Milltown,
Where trout enjoy their waters clear,
The rainbows, white and brown.

In thought I stand by the old blue gate
On an evening bright and still;
I hear the cuckoo and the corncrake
And the fox from a distant hill.

What kind of man could shape a plan
To place a dump in there
And incinerate the plastic waste
To pollute the atmosphere.

But they have made a stand for this lovely land
Where once the forest grew,
And to replant again would be their aim
The lands of the old coulew.

Tourists come and tourists go,
Even some come back to stay,
To see the views we have to show
And to walk the Dingle Way.

Have you ever been to the Teampall Geal
And looked inside the cave,
Where saintly men were forced to hide
When their only walk was Casán na Naomh.

Have our county planners got it wrong
Or is it just a few
Would use this historic scenic walk
To divide a dump in two.

So, Coiste na Coille must keep a watchful eye
To preserve this walk for another day,
For the generations yet to come
And Coláiste Ide not far away.

Three national monuments guard this place
St. Manchans is not alone,
For the Gates of Glory guard the East
And to the north the Kilfountain Stone.

So when they go on Easter Day
To pay the Holy Round,
They will ask their saint to save this place
From being a dumping ground.

Patrick O'Connor,
31/7/91

DINGLE'S OLD SEA WALL

Of the wall around Jerusalem all of you would know,
Or the Great Wall built in China many years ago,
But when the storm was coming and the glass began to fall,
There were many sought the shelter of Dingle's Old Sea Wall.

Have you ever looked across the harbour wall to view a harbour scene
Across the road from Flahive's Bar that fronts the Dingle Green,
See the College in the woodlands, the Esk tower and the Hut
And young lads picking winkles from the wall out to the foot.

This wall saw many changes as the tide did ebb and flow,
The Steamer and the Schooner and the Nobbies come and go,
The barrels of salted mackerel before we had deep freeze
And the flags of many nations that came floating in the breeze.

It saw how the ships were laden with timber, coal and grain,
The fish and pigs and cattle being loaded on the train,
It saw a T.D. and a Taoiseach for years they were on call,
It is then there was no danger to Dingle's Old Sea Wall.

It saw the fishing boats of Dingle as they came in one by one,
Out since the early morning until the setting sun,
When they tied up at their moorings with their catches big and small,
The tourist and the native could see them from the wall.

It gave protection to the farmers when they were passing there,
In the darkness of the morning, walking cattle to the fair,
And when the storm was raging, an old sea dog did recall
How he watched the Atlantic breakers roll back from that great wall.

When the Fungie boats go sailing out and more come sailing in,
A tourist in a wet suit going for a dolphin swim,
Or the day of the old regatta when the women wore the shawl,
When their oarsmen crossed the winning line they threw it on the wall.

Some boats were getting old now and some are obsolete,
So they made changes in the harbour for the new and better fleet,
A marina for the yachts with their masts so strong and tall,
So time was running out now for Dingle's Old Sea Wall.

Like Saint Patrick on the Hill of Slane, Peggy Flahive took a stand
And stood before the engineers with signatures in hand,
With the T.D. gone and Haughey gone, how could she hold the line,
So in fairness to the Council the wall had served its time.

When the morning sun was peeping over the mountains of the town,
And all the street was sleeping, the wall came tumbling down,
The new wall built not far away will let the traffic flow,
That is the price of progress, we were sad to see it go.

Patrick O'Connor   Oct. '93

PADDY BAWN BROSNAN

May the good Lord rest you Paddy Bawn
You have now passed away,
In late July of Ninety Five
On Munster Final Day.
When forty thousand packed the field
To see this Gaelic game,
Their heads they bowed, in silence stood,
In memory of your name.

From this mighty man in many ways
Our youth could take their cue,
On fishing grounds, in the sporting field
Or in the Sunday pew.
In Croke Park on All Ireland Day
As the Kingdom strove for Sam,
He showed the courage of the lion,
Yet the meekness of the lamb.

To the Green and Gold great honour brought,
And to his native town,
But now he walks with former greats
And peacefully looks down,
Where he can see the rising sun
Light up the new born day
Or watch the moon dispense its beams
O'er lovely Dingle Bay.

That bay he knew and loved so well
Going out or homeward bound,
He steered his boat 'round Skelligs
Or through the Blasket Sound.
He bravely faced the Atlantic wave
'Round Inisvicillane,
And watched the dolphin leaping high
Below the Toureen Bawn.

So we bid farewell to Paddy Bawn,
In his day he reigned supreme,
At fielding high and driving long
Or ploughing the ocean stream.
And when our team again sails forth
With courage and with pride,
Two eagle eyes will watch each move,
The Bawn will match each stride.

Patrick O'Connor.

THE BREWERY GATE
An ode to Dingle of years gone by

As I ramble back to my younger days
There are things I remember well,
Like the axial crack of the creamery car
And the ring of the criers bell.

Walking cattle to the fair
From their far away abode,
From Brandon Point, from Dun an Oir,
Till they reached the town's Spa Road.

Some had no money in their till
To pay their entry rate
But a wink of an eye from Tom the Boy
And they were in through the Brewery Gate.

The young lads took the cattle then
While the old one's went to rest
Across the road to Nellie and Fred
For a drink of the very best.

It was often said of Nellie and Fred,
Though they took things in their stride,
That they silenced the crack of the creamery car
With the craic that went on inside.

There were no grants for farmers then,
No talk of CAP or GATT,
But on the twenty first day they got their creamery pay
They drank to the butter fat.

Many a man dropped in for one,
Only to linger rather late,
While his flightly mare stood anxious there,
Hitched up to the Brewery Gate.

The Brewery Gate saw ducks and geese
And the best of all feathered stock
And every turkey hen from hill and glen
Came there to the turkey cock.

So, on Christmas Day as your turkey cooked
And you had all day long to wait
For that rare old bird you can have my word
That came through the Brewery Gate.

Many a man came to the Brewery
When the storm had passed by,
For many a roof was made water proof
With a box from Tom the Boy.

A Church event did one time change
The date of the monthly fair,
It was then the crier was called out
As there was no radio on the air.

Jim Crones he shouted out the change,
The change of time and date,
And the crier's bell rang loud and clear
Around the Brewery Gate.

The Mart has now replaced the fair,
The fairs we used to know,
And the Brewery Gate is a big lounge bar,
Call in to Kitty and Joe.

Patrick O'Connor.

"Here is the poem, written by Peig Sayers son, Mike-An File, in praise of Doctor Savage. He did so much for Dingle Hospital. It was he who brought it from a workhouse to a hospital and gave the people the hospital they have today."
                                        Sr. M. Columba Leen,
                                                Dingle Hospital.

DÓMHNALL UASAL Ó SÁMHÁIN

Rath Dé go raibh ar do lámh,
A chara na bhfíor- bhochtáin,
'S is trua gan Inis Fáil,
Lán ded' shórt gach uile lá.

Géag de'n ghlan-fhuil, d'easgair é,
Plannda gaile, árd a chéim,
Laoch do sheasaimh bearna an bhaoil,
Caoin le cara, is tais le tréith.

Sé Dómhnall uasal Ó Sámháin,
Dochtúir leighis tinn is slán,
Do bronnadh air san gheineamhain thuas
Buadh na mbuadh do bheith aige.

D' fhanfainn á mholadh gan scáth,
Ó líonadh go trágha de'n mhuir,
Ór ní lem' pheann do mholfainn an áig,
Acht le croí atá lán de chion.

Cion ó aois go bás,
Toirbhrím-se is cách duith,
Is dubhach liom gur geal an lá,
Gur sgaradh ód' chomhdháil sinn.

Dá mbeadh againn a shamhail siúd,
Is beag dár bpúir a bheadh ag gearán,
Mar fear chomh h-oilte leis ar an gcéird,
Ní fheichfeann len ár ré arís.

Dochtúir uasal, cneasta, séimh,
Múinte, béasach, banamhail, mín,
Curadh le cara, b'fholas é,
Ag dul i mbun a ghnóthaí go léir.

Nár leige Dia go bhráth
Géag chomh glan-chroidheach leis, ar seachrán,
Cé go bhfuil an saol so lán de'n olc,
A Chríost cuir cosc le gach droch ní.

An File

GLORIOUS, GLORIOUS SCHOOL DAYS

Glorious, glorious school days,
Happy of our life,
Till we never think so
Until we are struck in strife.

We can all remember baby days of old
When our mother guided us to the schoolroom door.
In Josephs class we sat at desk and often roused a scream,
Singing songs and making paper flowers.

From class to class we graded
Like young birds from a nest,
Already we have parted
With one of our best pals
God has seen us ready
For our home beyond the stars.

Just a few of us are left alone
And we are struggling on,
Just waiting, weary waiting,
For the future to come on.

Margaret O'Sullivan, Main St.

THE DINGLE PUCK GOAT

I am a young jobber, who's foolish and airy,
The green hills of Kerry I came for to see.
I went down to Dingle to buy up some cattle,
And I hope you will listen to what happened to me.
I entered the fair on a Saturday morning,
The first thing I met was a long legged goat,
Bedad then, says I, for to commence the dealing,
I think my old hero, you're worth a pound note.

This cute rascal dared me, he thought he could scare me,
That Dingle puck goat was a monster to see,
He wore a long meggal as grey as a badger,
That would reach from Dingle to Cahirciveen.
He'd a pair of long horns like any two bayonets,
And just like two needles were pointed on top,
And I am quite certain you would not be laughing
If he threw you aloft and caught you on the hop.

I made my acquaintance to the owner who held him,
A bargain we made without any delay.
Then he said, 'As you've paid me down twenty-two shillings
Some advice I'll give you before you go away.
This daring old fellow, he well knows the mountains,
In the year sixty four he first started to drill,
And some of his comrades, I'm told were transported,
Since then, he's determined some blood for to spill'.

The old man departed, and I too, had started,
That story he told me put me in despair:
The first jump the goat gave, near broke my left arm,
So I jumped on his back and caught hold of his hair.
Says I, my bold fellow, on your back I am landed,
Unless I fall off, you may go where you will'.
He ran through the streets like a puca distracted,
And soon made his way towards steep Conor Hill.

When we came into Brandon, I thought it was London,
I regretted my journey when I saw the sea.
He jumped in the water! He swam right across it,
And soon made his way towards Castlegregory.
The waves of the ocean set me in a motion,
The fishes, they ate all the nails off my toes,
And a very big mackerel jumped at my nostrils,
And I thought he'd make off with the bridge of my nose.

When we came to the seashore, he galloped quite hastily,
Towards Gleann na nGealt and Castlemaine he did stray,
Towards Milltown, Killorglin and into Killarney,
And never did stop till he came to Kenmare.
At length then, he spoke, saying, 'I've passed my headquarters,
The place where my ancestors always have been,
Then let us return, and we'll take up our lodgings
At Peggy na nGabhars where there's plenty poteen'.

When I heard the goat speaking, my heart commenced beating,
Says I, 'Tis a spirit or some demon cut loose,
Or something contrary, that strayed into Kerry,
Says I to myself, ' I am done wearing shoes'.
Then he returned and stayed there 'till morning,
And during the night I lay stretched on his back,
As morning was dawning, he jumped from his corner,
And towards Castleisland he went like a crack.

To the town of Tralee he next took his rambles,
I felt he was anxious to see some more sport.
Outside the town he met kilted Highlanders,
And he 'up' with his horns and tore all their clothes.
The Highlanders screamed, and they bawled 'míle murder',
Calling the peelers to put him in jail.
But the louder they ranted, the faster the goat ran,
And away helter-skelter he gave them leg bail.

When he jumped in the Basin, I fell on the footway,
Away went the goat and I saw him no more.
I suppose he's gone back to where he belongs to,
Or else he may stray to a far distant shore.
But if he's in Ireland 'tis in Camp or in Brandon,
Or away in the mountains in some place remote.
But whilst I am living I've a story worth telling
Of my rambles in Kerry and the Dingle Puck Goat.

Other verses:

The wisdom of sages, begor, 'Tare-an-ages',
Was put in the cranium of that old pucán,
Through fields he would scamper, without any wages,
Of onions or praties from dusk until dawn.
He'd break through all stables, he'd crash through all gables,
He'd smash all the tables, from here to Tralee.
He'd gallop like thunder, and, sure 'tis no wonder,
That Dingle Puck Goat was the finest you'd see.

He'd bate all the bailiffs, the Moguls, and Caliphs,
All the Shulers and Rulers from Cork to Baghdad.
He'd make them cut capers to put in the papers,
With one puck from his horns, he'd drive them all mad.
For that bright Saxon shilling he never was willing,
Still he'd go to the polls for old Ireland to vote;
From a fight ne'er relaxing, he was there for the axin',
That war-like old bucko, the Dingle Puck Goat.

THE YANKEE GENTLEMAN WHO SMOKED THE LONG CIGAR

The sun shone bright in Dingle,'twas a fair day in the town
And drinks were flowing freely in the harp above the crown
And all the farmers boys were there from Brandon to Tralee,
All changing gold in sovereigns and drinking whiskey free.

Now Mrs. Murphy's barmaids were hustling here and there
With steaming glass and flowing mug, rich odours filled the air,
Then as a ray of sunshine illumed the dusky bar,
In strolled a Yankee gentleman who smoked a long cigar.

Along the bar from man to man he glanced a roving eye,
Many a mile have I come said he, believe me I am dry,
So join me boys in what so e'er your favourite liquors are,
And we joined the Yankee gentleman who smoked the long cigar.

He owned us from that moment forth and then began "mo chroí",
A day like this I've never seen or never again hope to see,
We asked for friends in thousands in the land of stripes and stars,
He knew them all this gentleman who smoked the long cigar.

As Mrs Murphy's barmaid strolled past this gentleman
He tucked herself beneath the chin, come "Tabhair dom póg" said he,
No boy in all the barony such devilment would dare,
Yet when he asked her for that kiss her cheeks went rosy rare.

He raised a noggin to his lips, 'twas filled with sly poteen,
Here's to your dear old land, he said, who's fields are always green,
And here's to your lovely maidens too and he gave herself a wink,
And here's to your good whiskey and then he stopped to drink.

The sun went down over Dingle Town, the Yankee sighed to see,
He lit another long cigar and beat it for Tralee.
And oft since then,"A mhic mo chroí", where summer glides the glen,
We wonder will this gentleman, will he some time come again,
And still we toast with cup and can around Mrs. Murphy's bar
That pleasant spoken gentleman who smoked the long cigar.

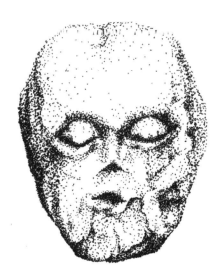

Crom Dubh

A CAOINEADH FOR CROM.

Crom Dubh was the pagan chieftain in Cloghane when Saint Brendan introduced Christianity to the area. Initially very hostile, he later became a generous benefactor of the new creed. In gratitude his effigy in stone was incorporated in Brendan's sixth century church and in the eleventh century church which replaced it. The stone head was stolen from the local churchyard in August 1993 and has not been recovered. The loss was deeply felt locally.

Go! Shout the awful tidings, spread the news from shore to shore,
Crom Dubh our chief is taken, we shall see him never more.
The father of our people, the guardian of our race,
The hero of our legends, he has vanished without trace.

While your people all lay sleeping, Great Crom, a thieving hand
Came and ripped you from the holy place where Brendan's chapel stands.
Sold like a slave for silver, betrayed for foreign gold,
Dishonoured among strangers who was king in days of old.

You bade farewell to Brendan when with oar and sail unfurled
He ploughed the wave to westward to seek out a newer world.
You welcomed back the sailor and mocked his traveller's tales
Of red-skinned men and ice and fire and great Atlantic whales.

You watched with bleak and stony eye when Viking raiders came
With fire and sword and terror they set the land aflame.
You suffered pain when Penal Laws our Faith and language banned
And the Wild Geese fled across the sea to fight in foreign lands.

You wept when grinding Famine held sway throughout the land,
And the dead uncoffined buried by their neighbours faltering hands.
The parents, gaunt as skeletons, who gasped with fevered breath,
Laid the sod upon their children and soon followed them in death.

The Fenian cry of Liberty rang in your ears of stone,
You knew when Roger Casement died in Pentonville alone.
You heard the tramp of armies when the nations fought their wars
And the thunder of the rockets as men sought to reach the stars.

For centuries before your eyes the generations passed
And father, son and grandchild came to rest by you at last.
In crumbling grave and tomb and vault the countless thousands lie,
You guarded their last resting place when came their day to die.

How oft on Crom Dubh Sunday, (I have heard the old people tell)
Have you watched the pilgrims praying at Saint Brendan's holy well.
The Pattern, and the dancing and the drinking and the throngs
The stalls piled high with goodies and the music and the songs.

Oh, woe betide the robber, he will live to rue the day,
For dark and deep and deadly is the curse of Crom they say.
A living death shall be his fate, the wages of his crime,
For your vengeance will pursue him down the corridors of time.

Paddy Moriarty.

ON THE SHORES OF BRANDON BAY

My love and I strayed hand in hand
At the closing of the day,
We saw the sun kiss the moon goodnight
On the shores of Brandon Bay;
On that peaceful strand, with the golden sand
Where the white waves gently play,
We saw the sun kiss the moon goodnight
On the shores of Brandon Bay.

The fuscia's flower sadly blooms,
By Kerry's mountain green,
The honeysuckle decks the hedge,
The wild rose in between;
The cuckoo calls, the skylark sings,
His brown wings upward soar
As he lifts his song to heaven there
By Brandon's peaceful shore.

The Mission bell tells Angelus
And bids the village pray,
The earnest priest says Holy Mass
At the closing of the day,
Good people all, confess your sins,
And give God praise and say,
I thank you Heavenly Father, for my
Home by Brandon Bay.

Though an Englishman I've an Irish heart
And I'm coming back some day
To see the sun kiss the moon goodnight
On the shores of Brandon Bay;
And when my time on earth is spent
Dear Lord, I ask no more
Than to let my tired body rest
By Brandon's peaceful shore.

And when my spirit upward flees
From wordly ties set free
And the gentle breeze on Brandon
Brings the secrets of the sea;
And when I reach the golden gates
Of the Heavenly Mansions free,
O Holy Mary, Mother dear,
Sweet Mary pray for me.

Rev. Arthur Wren,Carlisle. 1970

THE OLD POTHOLE ROAD FROM 'CASTLE TO CLOGHANE'.

Now did you hear the latest,
The news that's going around?
The bad state of our thoroughfare,
The likes was never found.
Yes the bad state of our thoroughfare
From 'Castle' to Cloghane,
Its nothing now but potholes,
We can hardly walk at all.

Now those who own the motor-cars,
Big road tax they must pay,
But now they're getting bankrupt
With expenses every day.
With punctured tyres and broken springs
They can hardly move at all
Along that road, that potholed road,
From 'Castle' to Cloghane.

Now nothing can keep up that road
But plenty of stones and tar
All flattened with the roller
And then you'll feel no jar.
It's a waste of all our money
Throwing loose stones here and there
But its good for Mr. Dunlop
And those who own a share.

Now, if they do not start to fix that road
We will have to shut it down
And telephone Aer Lingus
To take us to the town.
And then we'll build some aerodromes
Along that thoroughfare
Where she can stop and pick us up
And take us all by air.

Ned Moore

71

STRADBALLY

From Kerry's heathclad mountains
These lines I pen to you
Far away in exile
From these vales you loved to view,
And far from dear old comrades
You never more may see
That roamed the hills and valleys
With you in Stradbally.

How often summer evenings
As the sun was sinking low
Around the little hedgerows
Together we did go.
Our hearts were light and tender
From care we were quite free,
When we were here together
In sunny Stradbally.

But now we are divided
For its here you could not stay,
Like many more you were compelled
To wander far away.
To seek a home and livelihood
Far o'er the raging seas
And far from friends and neighbours
In dear old Stradbally.

I hope to meet you soon again
In this dear old land of ours,
I hope to meet you soon again
In this lovely land of flowers.
We'll talk about the happy past
And sing the songs of yore.
We'll settle down in Stradbally
To leave it never more.

SWEET KILCUMMEN

In sweet Kilcummen stands the cot where I've been,
It's close by the mountain where ripples the stream.
It's close by the mountain overlooking the sea
And that beautiful strand from Cloghane to Candiha.
Yes, that beautiful strand where the white waves do flow,
Where often I ramble when the north winds do blow.
Oh! Far have I travelled, many sights have I seen,
But none like the beauty around sweet Kilcumeen.

Now there every evening when the sun is going low
I can view all the canoes as fishing they go.
And from Brandon's high mountain to Loop Head in Clare
I can view from that cottage as I sit on my chair.
Yes, from Brandon's high mountain to Loop Head in Clare
Or beyond it to Galway the thought I declare,
Oh! Far have I travelled, many sights I have seen,
But none like the beauty around sweet Kilcumeen.

Now there every morning it's a pleasure to me
To sit down by the table drinking my tea,
The beautiful white waves as I said before,
All dashing and splashing they run for the shore.
Yes, dashing and splashing they never stay still,
They run up the strand and run down again.
Oh! Far have I travelled, many sights I have seen,
But none like the beauty around sweet Kilcumeen.

Now whenever I ramble away from that scene,
If it was but one night sure it's of it I dream.
And when home returning by the road to Cloghane
My heart it does open when I come to Goulane,
When I look all around me from Brandon to Clare
And the Maharee Islands abroad in the bay.
Oh! Far have I travelled, many sights have I seen,
But none like the beauty around sweet Kilcumeen.

Ned Moore

PORT YARROCK

In ninety three, July the sixth,
A gallant barque set sail
For Queenstown bound with orders
To cross the Atlantic main.

This vessel she was iron clad,
With copper she was laden,
Her sails were all tattered
Because she'd got no haven.

For two hundred days she braved the seas
And sad it was her lot,
That night she lay in Brandon Bay
Where no anchorage could be got.

Scarcely a week after
The winds began to flow,
The Port Yarrock drew her anchors
And into the seas did go.

The seas were raging furiously,
'Twas plain she could not stand
And when night approached she ran a wreck
Close by Kilcummin Strand.

Early the next morning,
At the hour of nine o' clock,
The waves rolled like mountains,
The ship she struck a bank.

The captain cried "Prepare me boys,
I fear we are all lost
And the only way to save our lives
Is to cling onto the mast".

Ah! Mournful was the scene
When the ship began to break,
And twenty human bodies
Into the deep were laid.

And as I gazed upon them,
As many on the shore,
No help or aid to come to save,
Alas! They are no more.

God help their poor relations
That they have left behind,
They're far away from Brandon Bay
Where sorrow they will find.

Where Captain Forbes and all his men
Close by the shore do lie,
May the Lord have mercy on their souls
For sudden they did die.

Now before I will lay down my pen
I have one word to say,
Let other men who do pass by
Remember Brandon Bay.

BRANDON BAY

A glorious summer sun arose above the ocean crest
And lightly kissed the murmuring streams and mountains of the west.
On blithesome wing the lark did sing and blackbirds piped their lay
When I left my home, being forced to roam from dear old Brandon Bay.

With tear-dimmed eyes I stood awhile to gaze on each dear scene
And cursed the fates that made me place long weary leagues between,
To catch Dame Fortune's fickle glance whose smile ne'er came my way,
I bid adieu to love and you, my dear old Brandon Bay.

Here 'midst the teeming multitudes a lonely man am I,
Each night beside the dim firelight alone I sit and sigh
And in my sleep I often weep and oft am heard to say,
My heart hath bled since the day I fled from dear old Brandon Bay.

There is not an hour that o'er me passed since last I saw her shore
That you are missing from my heart, you are treasured in its care.
No joy can heal the pain I feel nor pleasure steal away,
The memory fond linked with that land beside you, Brandon Bay.

Although perhaps my footsteps may never trace again,
The strand I loved in childhood, that lordly mountain chain,
Yet every throb my heart gives till life has passed away,
Is but a sigh to live and die beside you, Brandon Bay.

Den. Griffin.

Lines on the Fatal Railway Accident on the Dingle Railway on Whit-Monday.

What mean those awestruck faces ?
This hurrying to and fro ?
Those anxious eager questions,
What is it they want to know ?

Have you not heard the tidings,
   On lightning wires sped?
The Dingle Train ran off the line,
   And several men are dead.
To-day in distant Dingle
   Was held the Whitsun fair,
And many of our townsmen
   By a "special" travelled there;
And on the homeward journey,
   This illstarred afternoon,
The "special" rushed down Glen-na-galt,
   And hurled them to their doom.
You know that frightful incline,
   Right down the mountainside,
And at its base, the viaduct,
   That spans the foaming tide;
That tow'ring high arch'd structure,
   With its sudden horse-shoe curve,
Which makes ones heart to flutter,
   And tingles every nerve.
Well, down that awful hillside,
   To-day the special flew,
No human skill could stop her,
   Nor aught that man could do;
And those who saw that dreadful race,
   Declare with bated breath,
Their eyes shall ne'er shut out the sight
   Until they close in death.
They say they hear the mighty rush
   Far up the mountain side,

And wondered why the "special"
   Should make so fast a ride;
But as the sound grew nearer,
   Their hearts stood still in awe,
They knew such speed down Glen-na-galt
   Was disallowed by law,
Next moment round the winding curve
   The train dashed into view,
And towards the fateful viaduct
   She quick and quicker flew,
"She'll never round that sudden curve,
   Oh! What can be amiss?"
She leaped that instant from the rails
   Into the dread abyss.
A moment's awful stillness,
   And then, ye Gods, there came!
Up from that dreadful chasm,
   Appalling cries of pain;
And borne to the listeners ears,
   Were sounds of every kind;

The moans of human beings,
   And the yells of dying swine.
But eager feet soon reached the spot,
   And willing hands were found,
To lift the wounded from the wreck,
   And lay them on the ground;
Poor Redshaw, who was driver
   Of that ill-fated train,
Has made his final journey,
   He'll never drive again-
Whether by fault or accident,
   Controlling power was lost,
He felt like a brave soldier,
   And died at his post.
Poor Loughlin too and Dillon,
   Who shared the drivers fate,
Were far away from home and friends,
   And strangers at our gate.

Thank God, our friends and townsmen,
   Tho' bruised and mangled sore,
Were spared their lives, and with his help
   Will soon be as of yore.

Now drop the curtain softly
   On this heartrending scene,
And thank the Great Preserver
   'Tis not worse than it has been,
And while we offer up our thanks
   For friends spared to us here,
We'll breathe a kind God rest them
   O'er the strangers lonely bier.

J. Noble, R.I.C.,Tralee.1893

ANNASCAUL

O sweet Annascaul, on a bright summer's day,
The sunbeams shine fair on your flowerets so gay;
Your green tender valleys, maternal like hills,
Your clear placid river, your soft-singing rills.

A dreamer may dream or a sage find true rest,
By your scenic lake 'neath the hills of the West,
And a hermit of old, devoid of earth's care,
May have found here contentment in penance and prayer.

O far have I roamed from you, dear Annascaul,
But mem'ries of you I still fondly recall,
Of the scenes of my boyhood near lovely Inch strand,
Where the shells looked as jewels that I picked from the sand.

By the cliff-road I roved and gazed on the deep,
Where the waters oft would tire and then go to sleep,
And the air tasted honey as God's peace seemed to fall,
And no dark clouds or shadows fell o'er Annascaul.

Oh, your people are homely and kindly to meet,
To the poor they're generous, and strangers they'll greet,
While a céad míle fáilte and God bless you will fall,
From the lips of the colleens of old Annascaul.

T.P. Foran.1947

INCH OF HAPPY MEMORY

Oh! I have seen the sea at Inch,
The sand and hills and sky,
Nor will the memory from me part,
Until the day I die.

There's solace there for every mood,
And rest for weary brain,
The people there were very good,
And kind to travellers twain.

The golden sand there stretches fine,
Far as the eye can roam;
The sun's caresses make it shine,
Before 'tis kissed by foam.

The little curly ripples there,
Come wrinkling up the sand,
And wee folk love the feel of them,
'Tween bare toes on the strand.

Some days there is a deeper sound,
When winds blow from the hills around,
There's thunder in the League's fall,
When wild sea-horses call.

At night when all the world's a-nod,
The moonlit sea is tireless still,
Making sweet symphonies at will,
For the sleepless mind of God.

Oh! There is peace for soul of man,
And wisdom's deepest lore,
In the blissful charms of lovely Inch,
Sure Heaven has blest her shore.

Visitors at Inch, 1929.

THE BARREL OF RUM

'Tis long we will remember the year of '43,
A storm it was raging in the month of January,
The twenty fifth day of that month, at three o' clock that day,
A barrel was seen floating on the waves of Dingle Bay.

A few young men had watched it well as it did float along,
Their only grief would be to see it broken on the rocks,
But swiftly it soon made the shore in the current, wave and breeze,
And landed in a cliff below that village called Doonties.

The saving of the barrel is the next I will relate,
The task being not so easy in the storm, wind and rain,
But when they had it well secured to bore it they did come,
And the Doonties men soon drank a health from that barrel of strong rum.

To share the rum between them all they quickly did agree,
With all the vessels they could find, they hastily did proceed,
The night was dark and the lights were bad but the scuttling had been done,
With jars and cans and creamery tanks they drew it to the dump.

Before the night was over the Roasters gave a call,
And down below in Davy Jones they were greeted there by Tall,
They drank their 'nough and they all got tough, you could see them roll and fall,
They won't forget the night they spent in Faill a Tónacháin.

With buckets too the rum they drew along the rocky shore,
And with a dish came Mickey Fitz and the postman from Banogue,
Gur and Curráin, Tadhg and Tomás and that sailor boy T.A.,
To lead the boys with the rum that night was their famous Captain Tall.

Rabin too, I heard for sure, in Acres got the smell,
And with his pal, Tadhg Foran, in the search of rum they went,
They first attacked the Lackens back and right below Greenfields
They found a jar and down by Minard they quickly did retreat.

They crossed the Gub and they drank their 'nough as they thought
    they were not seen,
Along the coast they scrambled home by the southern shores of Reen,
And in the uplands by Glen's Hill their paradise had been,
They stayed that night in the booze, oh boy's, in Kilmurry by the sea.

The Guards and Tecs soon made a search in the village of Doonties,
They searched the village east and west from Griffins to Greenfields,
With spears and pikes of every type they tossed the heaps of dung,
But to their surprise they did not find that barrel of strong rum.

Cronin and Guard Folen were the leaders of the raid,
They searched the fields and hedges and the houses everywhere,
They swore that if they would find the rum the Doonties would get jail,
But the Doonties men pitched them to Hell for they knew the rum was safe.

I hope me boys ye will enjoy those verses I have sung,
And when we'll meet I hope you'll greet me with a glass of rum,
If ever you roam the Doontie road and if your drinking call
Into Mike's, to Tall's or Tadhg's or even Johnny Curráin's.

The rum running is over now and I have no more to say,
The people are still watching the coast by night and by day,
Young and old are on patrol from Greenfields to the Gub
And anxiously are waiting for another cask of rum.

Seán O'Sullivan, Glen Minard

THERE ARE MANY HARBOURS NEAR OUR SHORE

There are many harbours near our shore,
From Galway Bay to Baltimore,
One of the finest harbours man could see
Is the pleasant harbour of Ventry.

This pleasant harbour is broad and wide,
Fine and calm on the western side,
For ships that run in from the stormy sea
Into the safe harbour of Ventry.

Near this harbour there is the finest strand,
A fine shore and a fertile land,
There was a great battle here long ago
Near the waters down below.

Those great heroes were on the strand,
Between the harbour and the land,
This great battle was near the sea
On the strand of Ventry.

This fine harbour is wide and deep,
Where the flat-fish and the herring sleep.
There were great fishermen there long ago
From Cuas Cromtha to Ballymore.

Around this harbour there is a fine shore,
From Ventry to Ballymore,
Of all the harbours of the west
Ventry harbour is the best.

BY SLEA HEAD

A sudden quiet came o'er the happy group,
As winding road climbed up the wind swept slope.
The top displayed a gorge from sky to sea,
Round which the rock-hewn road clung gingerly.

Midway a stream from mountain glen roared down,
And o'er the road bed wildly tore its way:
Then leaped in mad abandon through a gap,
Where hungry seas prank up each frothy drop.

Through twisting headlands cautiously we tread,
To view the awful grandeur of Slea Head;
And we so bound by friendship - drift apart,
That undisturbed we feast our eyes and heart.

Vast pyramids of rock rear up to pierce the sky,
Some where a lost lamb bleats, as wild birds cry;
Dame nature's fortress - dreadful majesty,
Defying both storm and sea eternally.

A downward glance as we stand on the brink,
Our courage fails - instinctively we shrink;
Tormented seas tear madly at the base,
But, impotent, retreat in full disgrace.

The Blasket Islands crowned with bridal mist,
That vanishes when by the sun's rays is kissed;
Deserted and forlorn they wonder where
Have gone the joyful folks of yesteryear.

Ten leagues away the Skelligs reach the sky,
Where monks did penance in the days gone by;
Their evening hymns re-echoing o'er the sea,
Called home fish-laden boats rowed wearily.

We see huge ocean liners cleave the ocean blue,
For countless thousands this was their last view;
And well they know few will return some day
And feel they're lucky though they're bent and grey.

But they who leave don't go away in vain,
As Ireland's loss becomes the world's gain;
They bring the light of Faith to infidel
As round the world they weave a magic spell.

The turf fire burns low, its time for bed,
Then comes a parting blessing from each friend;
And then a prayer from both our hearts ashore,
Thank God, at last, we're home forever more.

Louis Baker, New York.

MY HOME IN GORTADOO

When I cross the Bridge of Blennerville, and turn my face back West,
My pulse it races faster, and my heart leaps in my breast,
I'm back in Corca Dhuibhne now my rambling days all through,
On the road to Ballyferriter, and my home in Gortadoo.

Through Camp, I go,and Gleann na nGealt and far famed Annascaul,
And I think of Crean of Antarctica where Scott the Brave did fall,
I'm near my goal when I reach Lispole soon Dingle Bay is in view,
On the last leg of my journey to my home in Gortadoo.

When I leave the Bóthar Fada, then from Baile na nDá I see,
Where Mount Brandon stands in high command above the Sisters Three,
The furze are yellow bonfires 'gainst the purple heathers hue,
As through misty eyes I recognise my home in Gortadoo.

Tá Gaoluinn bhinn le cloisint fós i mbéal na ndaoine ann,
Flaithúlacht agus comharsanacht, cuideachta, sport 'is greann,
An lon dubh is an smólach, iad ag scaipeadh lén is cumha,
Táim arís i mbláth m'óige 's mé ar ais ar na Gorta Dubha.

An fuscia dearg álainn ar an ngliotar 'Deora Dé,
Na fuiseoga maidin Earraigh ag cur Gailet roimh an ngréin,
Ar giorra mear, an easin mín, an chuach's an sionnach rua,
Taid go léir le feiscint ann thiar ar na Gorta Dubha.

As I watch the Autumn slanting sun set by my cottage door,
Fond thoughts come coursing through my mind of friends I'll see no more,
So lay me down in Dunurlinn amid neighbours kind and true,
Where one and all we'll wait God's call from our homes in Gortadoo.

So raise up your glass, each lad and lass, and drink a toast with me,
To each hill and vale around Ceann Sibéal, to Dún Chaoin by the sea,
My hearts desire to which I aspire I'll now disclose to you,
That I'd like to see old Ireland free in my home n Gortadoo.

Garry McMahon.

A SONG FOR THE BOOLTEEN

I'm here in Massachusetts now three thousand miles from home,
But my heart is back in old Ireland far across the raging foam
In a spot in County Kerry where I left when scarce eighteen,
On the map its Ballyferriter but we called it the Boolteen.

At the foot of Cruach Mharthain, where it nestles in the lee,
Of the south west wind that funnels in from the broad Atlantic sea,
To school we went to, barefoot then, each buachaill and cailín,
My heart broke in two when I bid adieu to my love and the Boolteen.

Bhfuil an Gaoluinn bhinn á labhairt acu ag geata an séipéal,
Is conas tá Baile Uachtarach ag bun Ceann Geal Sibéal,
Bhfuil tóir ar tigh an tSaorsaigh fós is ar tabhairne Danalín,
Bheinn sona sámh le piúnt im lámh i gceart lár an Bhuailtín.

To stand once more at Granville's door and see that pleasant view,
Smerwick Harbour and Mount Brandon, framed by flowers of every hue,
The gannets diving in the bay, the seagulls cry and keen
As home they fly in the clear blue sky above my own Boolteen.

My brother Dan sends the Kerryman tied up in a special fold,
It brings me all the news of home, although its three weeks old.
I call to mind the happy times we hunted the dreoilín,
How we laughed and sang as the rafters rang in the pubs of the Boolteen.

My trunks are packed, my passage paid, I leave tomorrow week,
My pension stout should see me out as my native land I seek.
I'll pick wild mushrooms once again on your dewy fields so green
And walk Béal Bán at break of dawn 'till I'm called from the Boolteen.

Garry McMahon.

THE LAND OF THE GAEL

I wish I was westward of Dingle on the golden sands of Béal Bán
Where I'd wait for the mountain of Brandon, to appear in the red
   light of dawn,
I'd gaze over Smerwick Harbour, see the yacht with its billowing sail,
My body is here in the Bowery, but my heart's in the Land of the Gael.

For the curse of the drink is upon me, it softens my will and my brain,
And as soon as I save a few dollars, I fall of the wagon again,
But I'm thinking of lovely Cruach Mharthain, the Blaskets and fair
   Ceann Sibéal,
When the sun is a red ball of fire, as it sets on the Land of the Gael.

In my mind's eye I see every detail, her mountains and valleys and seas,
The butterfly dancing a hornpipe, the thistledown flying in the breeze,
The fuscia, loosestrife and cowparsley, the primrose that blooms in
   the vale,
I'll pick the wild flowers in the Summer time when I'm back in the
   Land of the Gael.

The wind like a knife it goes through me and with hunger I'm ready
   to fall,
And the snowflakes are swirling around me as I head for the Church
   Mission Hall,
I hear the sweet song of the skylark, and list to the curlew's sad wail,
As over the ocean they call me to come back to the land of the Gael.

For it's forty long years since I left it, a young fellow still in my teens,
Did I ever return now you ask me,I go back every night in my dreams,
Yes the call of my homeland's all powerful, and I'm certain this time
   I'll not fail,
Then I'll hear the old tongue and again I'll be young when I'm home
   in the Land of the Gael.

Garry McMahon.

COME LISTEN HERE MY TRUSTY FRIENDS

Come listen here my trusty friends and I'll sing for you a song.
Its all about those hardy lads, I won't delay you long.
They left their homes that morning with spirits light and gay.
Sure, its well they knew their arms would win the honour of the day.

They stepped into their canvas boat and soon gave her a name.
Ned Moriarty then he did strip off and the others did the same.
They never put down their dulpins, this brave and daring four.

The Cuas canoe then came in view, no doubt they were good men.
But as for to beat those hardy lads, they should be as good again.
The Reneigh canoe then turned up, likewise the Reneigh four.
They also came to bring the race and put down Ballymore.

And when the race was started, Ned Moriarty took the lead.
And Cleary cried we'll keep it boys, we'll show them of what we're made.
They turned the pole most gallantly, those brave and daring four.
And Paddy Neill then shouted, we'll hold it Ballymore.

John Fitz said to his companions as he sat on the Conquerors bow,
We never yet were beaten and we won't be beaten now.
We'll sweep her off the water as we often did before,
And the Conqueror must bring the race to Cousheen Ballymore.

The Conqueror she came in first, Cuas and Reneigh were surprised.
The truth I am telling you.
Each thought their own four were the best, the best to catch an oar.
But the hardy lads are living yet in Cousheen Ballymore.

When the conquerors came into the slip, the people gathered round.
To welcome those brave hardy four, their match cannot be found.
They came in like heroes as they often did before.
And we drank their health on Monday night in Cousheen Ballymore.

Good luck to those hardy lads where ever they may go.
They are a credit to this place as the people all may know.
They have the hearts of Irishmen as everybody knows.
They are a credit to their people and to Cousheen Ballymore.

The tricolours were to be seen along the conquerors bow.
Although the paint had been rather fresh, it was washed off by the tide.
For the next regatta she is prepared, with green she is painted o'er,
And the like of her will not be seen with her crew from Ballymore.

Their trainers Eugene, likewise Moriarty John,
And also Pat Griffin, that big and sponky man.
Next comes Maurice Cleary, we'll finish up the crew,
With Neill and Batt and the Gearaltrac, they were all from Ballymore.

Seán MacGearailt, Baile Mór.

DINGLE BAY

You can hear God's Angels singing,
All the night and all the day,
Sure! You're just next door to heaven,
When you come to Dingle Bay.

Here's all of life's best happiness;
And the peace for which men pray,
In the laughter round the firesides
Within a town by Dingle Bay.

A hundred, thousand, million times
I'm dreaming of the day,
While the heart of me is crying
For a glimpse of Dingle Bay.

But after all - "Heaven on Earth",
You're not so far away:
I fold my hands, close my eyes
And wake up in Dingle Bay.

Gerald Fox

FOR THE READER

Sympathetic friend I'll dry my pen
And leave Dingle's praises to other men,
I described the scenes as best I could,
From Beenbawn Head to Burnham wood.

The scholastic pedant bent on faults to find
Can dismiss them as products of the rustic mind,
For my efforts I'll win no great renown,
For no man is a prophet in his native town.

The fine old customs we practise year by year,
To us are cherished still and dear,
After a time I fear they will fade away,
Like the silken petalled primroses of May.

Brendan Foley

Thanks to:

Jackie Ashe; Pat Ashe; Michael Collins; Tim Collins; Michael Costello; Cáit Curley; Annie Curran; David & Mary Donegan; Geraldine Fox; Pat Fox; Eileen Galvin; Dan Graham; Timmy Kelliher; Sr. M. Columba Leen; Danny Lynch, New York; Paidí Mhárthain Mac Gearailt; Canon Jack McKenna; John Benny Moriarty; Paddy Moriarty; Ted Moriarty; Garry McMahon; Kathleen Murphy, Dingle Library; Ríonach Uí Ógáin; Michael O'Connor; Pat O'Connor; Patrick O'Connor; Fergus Ó Flaithbheartaigh; David & Helena O'Mahony; Johnny O'Neill; Joan Rohan; Jim Twomey, FÁS Multimedia.

Kerryman (microfilm records Kerry County Library)

Dómhnall Uasal Ó Sámháin; There Are Many Harbours Near Our Shore(IFC1712:42-3); Come Listen Here My Trusty Friends (IFC S424:224-8) courtesy Dept of Irish Folklore.